UNCOMMON PRAYERS

UNCOMMON PRAYERS

COLLECTED BY CECIL HUNT

American Edition arranged by

JOHN WALLACE SUTER

1955 · GREENWICH · CONNECTICUT

PREFACE

In his three compilations, UNCOMMON PRAYERS, MORE UNCOMMON PRAYERS, and UNCOMMON PRAYERS FOR YOUNG PEOPLE, Mr. Cecil Hunt gathered into three books prayers from widely differing authors and countries and periods. That these volumes received a warm welcome from readers of varying traditions and faiths, from the orthodox as well as the sceptical, will be no surprise to those whose first acquaintance with his work is made in the pages of the present volume.

In selecting for an American edition prayers from all three of the original books, the editor has aimed at preserving the special qualities which distinguished Mr. Hunt's compilership: a breadth of outlook, and a sense of humor. That the latter trait should manifest itself in so serious an enterprise as prayer does not in fact present us with a paradox, for humor is an aspect of proportion, which in turn is an element of prayer—wisely defined as "the art of taking everything into consideration." This, of course, as the derivation of the word suggests, means taking everything outdoors and thinking about it under the stars.

To aid the reader in finding what he wants when he wants it, the prayers have been grouped roughly according to subject. This seemed better than to arrange them into three chapters representing the original books. It is hoped that the present volume may achieve by this plan a unity not otherwise obtainable. There is, however, no attempt made at didacticism; any such motive would defeat the purpose of Mr. Hunt's compilations: to present to the reader, without comment or interference, expressions of prayer which have welled up in the hearts of sincere persons of many cultures and in many lands.

John Wallace Suter

CONTENTS

ONE

PRAYER

Lord, teach us to pray.

Luke xi. 1

Thou art my wisdom; Thou knowest me as I am.

À KEMPIS

LORD, I know not what I ought to ask of Thee; Thou only knowest what I need.

Thou lovest me better than I know how to love myself.

O Father, give to Thy child that which he himself knows not how to ask. . . .

I simply present myself before Thee; I open my heart to Thee. . . . Behold my needs which I know not myself; see, and do according to Thy tender mercy. Smite, or heal; depress me, or raise me up. I adore all Thy purposes without knowing them; I am silent, I offer myself in sacrifice, I yield myself to Thee.

I would have no other desire than to accomplish Thy will. Teach me to pray; pray Thyself in me.

François Fénelon, Archbishop, 1651-1715

3

O Lord our God, teach us, we beseech Thee, to ask Thee aright for the right blessing. Steer Thou the vessel of our life towards Thyself, Thou tranquil Haven of all storm-tossed souls. Show us the course wherein we should go. Renew a willing spirit in us. Let Thy Spirit curb our wayward senses, and guide and enable us into that which is our true good, to keep Thy laws, and in all our works evermore to rejoice in Thy glorious and gladdening Presence. For Thine is the glory and praise from all Thy saints for ever and ever.

St. Basil, 329-379

The words that make a man feel strong in speaking
Truth.   TENNYSON

HEAR us, O hear us, Lord; to Thee
A sinner is more music, when he prays,
    Than spheres' or angels' praises be,
In panegyric allelujahs;
        Hear us, for till Thou hear us, Lord,
        We know not what to say;
Thine ear to our sighs, tears, thoughts, gives voice and
        word;
O Thou who Satan heard'st in Job's sick day,
Hear Thyself now, for Thou in us dost pray.

                              John Donne, 1572-1631

In all our prayers, th'Almighty does regard
The judgment of the balance, not the yard:
He loves not words, but matter; 'tis His pleasure
To buy His wares by weight, and not by measure.

                         Francis Quarles, 1592-1644

*O come hither, and hearken, all ye that fear God; and
I will tell you what he hath done for my soul.*

PSALM LXVI. 14

HAVE you no words! Ah, think again,
Words flow apace when you complain,
And fill your fellow-creature's ear
With the sad tale of all your care.

Were half the breath thus vainly spent,
To heaven in supplications sent;
Your cheerful song would off'ner be,
"Hear what the Lord has done for me!"

William Cowper, 1731-1800

The sure relief of prayer.

WORDSWORTH

Be not afraid to pray; to pray is right.
Pray, if thou canst, with hope; but ever pray,
Though hope be weak, or sick with long delay.
Pray in the darkness, if there be no light.
Far is the time, remote from human sight,
    When war and discord on the earth shall cease;
    Yet every prayer for universal peace
    Avails the blessed time to expedite.

Whate'er is good to wish, ask that of Heaven,
Though it be what thou canst not hope to see:
Pray to be perfect, though material leaven,
Forbid the spirit so on earth to be;
    But if for any wish thou dar'st not pray,
    Then pray to God to cast that wish away.

Ernest Hartley Coleridge, 1769-1849

The Lord is King: be the world never so unquiet.

Let all mortal flesh keep silent, and with fear and
trembling stand;
Ponder nothing earthly-minded, for with blessing in His
hand,
Christ our God to earth descendeth, our full homage to
command.

Liturgy of St. James

The prayers I make will then be sweet indeed,
If Thou the spirit give by which I pray:
My unassisted heart is barren clay,
That of its native self can nothing feed.

Michael Angelo, 1475-1564

Prayer is a powerful thing, for God has bound and tied Himself thereto.   LUTHER

> PRAYER is the soul's sincere desire,
>   Uttered or unexpressed;
> The motion of a hidden fire
>   That trembles in the breast.
>
> Prayer is the burden of a sigh,
>   The falling of a tear,
> The upward glancing of an eye
>   When none but God is near.
>
> Prayer is the simplest form of speech
>   That infant lips can try;
> Prayer the sublimest strains that reach
>   The Majesty on high.
>
> Prayer is the contrite sinner's voice,
>   Returning from his ways,
> While Angels in their songs rejoice,
>   And cry, "Behold, he prays!"
>
> Prayer is the Christian's vital breath,
>   The Christian's native air,
> His watchword at the gates of death:
>   He enters heaven with prayer.
>
> O Thou by whom we come to God,
>   The Life, the Truth, the Way,
> The path of prayer Thyself hast trod:
>   Lord, teach us how to pray.

J. Montgomery, 1771-1854

Shutting out Fear with all the strength of Hope.

BROWNING

O GOD our Father, who dost exhort us to pray, and who dost grant what we ask, if only, when we ask, we live a better life; hear me, who am trembling in this darkness, and stretch forth Thy hand unto me; hold forth Thy light before me; recall me from my wanderings; and, Thou being my Guide, may I be restored to myself and to Thee.

St. Augustine, 354-430

O MY Lord! If I worship Thee from fear of hell, burn me in hell; and if I worship Thee from hope of Paradise, exclude me thence; but if I worship Thee for Thine own sake, then withhold not from me Thine Eternal Beauty.

An Ancient Moslem Prayer

So may it happen unto me, and may I deserve it.

À KEMPIS

COME, Light serene and still;
Our darkened spirits fill
    With Thy clear day.
Guide of the feeble sight,
Star of grief's darkest night,
Reveal the path of right,
    Show us Thy way.

Traditional French Prayer, eleventh century

Thy will be done, though in my own undoing.

SIR THOMAS BROWNE

AND SO I sometimes think our prayers
   Might well be merged in one;
And nest and perch and hearth and church
   Repeat "Thy will be done!"

John Greenleaf Whittier, 1807-1892

My heart may find its peace in Thee.

À KEMPIS

RENEW my will from day to day,
Blend it with Thine, and take away
All that now makes it hard to say,
    "Thy will be done!"

Charlotte Elliott, 1789-1871

Whatever is wanting to me do Thou deign to supply.

À KEMPIS

AMEN, amen, amen!
So be it, Lord; we pray.
Whate'er Thy will for us
Each day,
Let us with thankful heart still say:
Amen, amen, amen!

T. T.

A CHILD may say amen
To a bishop's prayer, and feel the way it goes.

Elizabeth Barrett Browning, 1806-1861

TWO

IN HIS PRESENCE

Seek ye my face. . . . Thy face, Lord, will I seek.

Psalm xxvii. 7

Make that possible to me, O Lord, by grace, which ap-
pears impossible to me by nature.   À KEMPIS

HEAR, O Lord, when I cry with my voice:
Have mercy also upon me, and answer me.
When Thou saidst, Seek ye my face; my heart said unto
    Thee,
Thy face, Lord, will I seek.
Hide not Thy face from me;
Put not Thy servant away in anger:
Thou hast been my help;
Cast me not off, neither forsake me, O God of my salva-
    tion.

Teach me Thy way, O Lord;
And lead me in a plain path.

Wait on the Lord:
Be strong, and let thine heart take courage;
Yea, wait thou on the Lord.

                                        Psalm xxvii

Acquaint now thyself with him, and be at peace.

JOB xxii. 21

O ETERNAL Light, shine in our hearts;
O eternal Goodness, deliver us from evil;
O eternal Power, be Thou our support;
Eternal Wisdom, scatter the darkness of our ignorance;
Eternal Pity, have mercy upon us.

Grant unto us that with all our hearts, and minds, and strength, we may evermore seek Thy face; and finally, in Thy mercy, bring us to Thy holy presence. So strengthen our weakness that, following in the footsteps of Thy blessed Son, we may obtain Thy mercy and enter into Thy promised joy.

Alcuin, 735-804

If you seek yourself, you will find yourself, and that to your own ruin.

À KEMPIS

MANKIND can be, in fact, divided into three categories —those who find God and serve Him—those who, not having found Him as yet, are seeking for Him—and those who have neither found nor yet seek.

The first are sensible and happy—the second sensible and unhappy—the last are unhappy and mad.

From Pascal: The Man and the Message,
Roger H. Soltau

This is the highest wisdom.

À KEMPIS

I BELIEVE, O Lord, in Thee,
Father, Word, Spirit, One God.
That by Thy fatherly love and power all things were
   created;
That by Thy goodness and love to man
All things have been gathered together in one in Thy
   Word,
Who for us men and for our salvation was made
   flesh. . . .
This most holy faith which was once delivered to the
   Saints
I believe, O Lord; help Thou mine unbelief.

Lancelot Andrewes, Bishop, 1555-1626

Thou art my hope, my confidence, and my comforter.

À KEMPIS

WRITE Thy blessed name, O Lord, upon my heart, there to remain so engraven that no prosperity, no adversity, shall ever move me from Thy love.

Be Thou to me a strong Tower of defence,

A Comforter in tribulation,

A Deliverer in distress,

A very present Help in trouble, and

A Guide to heaven through the many temptations and dangers of this life.

Thomas à Kempis, 1380-1471

MAY the strength of God pilot us.

May the power of God preserve us.

May the wisdom of God instruct us.

May the hand of God protect us.

May the way of God direct us.

May the shield of God defend us.

May the host of God guard us against the snares of the Evil One and the temptations of the world.

May Christ be with us. Christ before us.

Christ in us. Christ over us.

May Thy salvation, O Lord, be always ours this day and for evermore.

St. Patrick, fourth century

My strength is made perfect in weakness.

II CORINTHIANS xii. 9

CHRIST, as a light,
Illumine and guide me!
Christ, as a shield, o'ershadow and cover me!
Christ be under me! Christ be over me!
Christ be beside me
On left hand and right!
Christ be before me, behind me, about me!
Christ this day be within and without me!

James Clarence Mangan, 1803-1849

MAY the defence of the Most High be above and beneath, around and within us, in our going out and in our coming in, in our rising up and in our going down, all our days and all our nights, until the dawn when the Son of Righteousness shall arise with healing in His wings for the people of the world, through Jesus Christ Our Lord.

Prayer used before Arnhem by the Parachute Regiment and inscribed in their Roll of Honour in St. Martin-in-the-Fields

I am the Rewarder of all who are good.

À KEMPIS

O FOUNTAIN of Love, love Thou our friends and teach them to love Thee with all their hearts, that they may think and speak and do only such things as are well-pleasing to Thee, through Jesus Christ our Lord.

St. Anselm, 1033-1109

WE beseech Thee, O Lord, remember all for good; have mercy upon all, O God. Remember every soul who, being in any trouble, stands in need of Thy mercy and help; all who are in need or distress; all who love or hate us.

Thou, O Lord, art the Helper of the helpless, the Hope of the hopeless, the Saviour of them who are tossed with tempests, the Haven of them who sail. Be Thou All to all. . . . Prosper Thou the work of our hands upon us; Oh, prosper Thou our handy-work.

Lord, be Thou within me, to strengthen me;
Without me, to keep me;
Above me, to protect me;
Beneath me, to uphold me;
Before me, to direct me;
Behind me, to keep me from straying;
Round about me, to defend me.
Blessed be Thou, O Lord, our Father, for ever and ever.

Lancelot Andrewes, Bishop, 1555-1626

*When you think yourself far off, I am often very near
to you.* À KEMPIS

FATHER of all, to Thee,
We breathe unuttered fears
Deep-hidden in our souls,
That have no voice but tears;
Take Thou our hand and through the wild
Lead gently on each trustful child.

J. Julian, nineteenth century

OUR courteous Lord willeth that we should be as
homely with Him as heart may think or soul may desire.
But let us beware that we take not recklessly this homeli-
ness as to leave courtesy.

Lady Julian of Norwich, 1343-1443

To be loved in preference to all.

My God, what is a heart,
That Thou shouldst it so eye, and woo,
Pouring upon it all Thy art,
As if Thou hadst nothing else to do?

Teach me Thy love to know;
That this new light, which now I see,
May both the work and workman show;
Then by a sunbeam I will climb to Thee.

George Herbert, 1593-1633

Sweet is e'en sorrow, coming in His name,
   Nor will I seek its purpose to explore,
His praise will I continually proclaim,
   And bless him evermore.

Abraham ibn Ezra, 1092-1167

And his heart was lifted up.

II CHRONICLES xvii. 6

THE saint, who walk'd on waves, securely trod
While he believ'd the beck'ning of his God.
But, when his faith no longer bore him out,
Began to sink, as he began to doubt.

John Dryden, 1631-1700

THAT, through these Labyrinths, not by groveling Wit,
But thy Silk-twist, let down from Heaven to me;
Did both conduct, and teach me, how by it,
To climb to thee.

George Herbert, 1593-1633

26

God does not deceive you; he is deceived who trusts too much to himself.
À KEMPIS

O LORD, I commend to Thee,
My soul and body,
My mind and my thoughts,
My prayers and my vows,
My senses and my limbs,
My words and my works,
My life and my death;
My friends, my benefactors, my well-wishers,
Those who have a claim on me;
My kindred and my neighbours,
My country and all Christendom.

Lancelot Andrewes, Bishop, 1555-1626

HEAR me, O God!
A broken heart
Is my best part:
Use still Thy rod,
That I may prove
Therein Thy love.

If Thou hadst not
Been stern to me
But left me free,
I had forgot
Myself and Thee.

Ben Jonson, 1572-1637

I give Thee thanks for Thy exceeding love.

À KEMPIS

To Mercy, Pity, Peace and Love
All pray in their distress;
And to these virtues of delight
Return their thankfulness.

For Mercy, Pity, Peace and Love
Is God, our Father dear,
And Mercy, Pity, Peace and Love
Is man, His child and care.

William Blake, 1757-1827

No man doth well but God hath part in him.

SWINBURNE

God be in my head,
    And in my understanding;
God be in my eyes,
    And in my looking;
God be in my mouth,
    And in my speaking;
God be in my heart,
    And in my thinking;
God be at my end,
    And at my departing.

Old Sarum Primer, 1558

GRANT me, I beseech Thee, Almighty and most Merciful God, fervently to desire, wisely to search out, and perfectly to fulfil all that is well-pleasing unto Thee.

Order Thou my worldly condition to the glory of Thy name; and, of all that Thou requirest me to do, grant me the knowledge, the desire and the ability, that I may so fulfil it as I ought, and may my path to Thee, I pray, be safe, straightforward and perfect to the end.

Give me, O Lord, a steadfast heart, which no unworthy affection may drag downwards; give me an unconquered heart, which no tribulation can wear out; give me an upright heart, which no unworthy purpose may tempt aside.

Bestow upon me also, O Lord my God, understanding to know Thee, diligence to seek Thee, wisdom to find Thee, and a faithfulness that may finally embrace Thee.

St. Thomas Aquinas, c. 1225-1274

For the obedience of faith.

ROMANS XVI. 26

O GOD, who hast commanded us to be perfect, as Thou art perfect; put into my heart, I pray Thee, a continual desire to obey Thy holy will. Teach me day by day what Thou wouldst have me to do, and give me grace and power to fulfil the same. May I never from love of ease, decline the path which Thou pointest out, nor, for fear of shame, turn away from it.

Henry Alford, 1810-1871

Prayer purifies; it is a self-preached sermon.

JEAN PAUL

GOD grant me
The serenity to accept the things I cannot change,
The courage to change the things I can,
And the wisdom to distinguish the one from the other.

Reinhold Niebuhr

His truth shall be thy shield and buckler.

PSALM XCI. 4

I PRAY thee, Lord, the Father, and the Guide of our reason, that we may remember the nobleness with which Thou hast adorned us; and that Thou would'st be always on our right hand and on our left, in the motion of our own wills; that so we may be purged from the contagion of the body and the affections of the brute, and overcome them and rule, and use, as it becomes men to use them, for instruments. And then that Thou would'st be in Fellowship with us for the careful correction of our reason, and for the conjunction by the light of truth with the things that truly are.

And in the third place, I pray Thee the Saviour, that Thou would'st utterly cleanse away the closing gloom from the eyes of our souls, that we may know well who is to be held for God, and who for mortal.

Last prayer of George Chapman, 1559-1634

A merry heart maketh a cheerful countenance.

PROVERBS XV. 13

O GOD, animate us to cheerfulness. May we have a joyful sense of our blessings, learn to look on the bright circumstances of our lot, and maintain a perpetual contentedness. Preserve us from despondency and from yielding to dejection. Teach us that nothing can hurt us if, with true loyalty of affection, we keep Thy commandments and take refuge in Thee.

William E. Channing, 1780-1842

Thy grace strengthening me.

À KEMPIS

ALMIGHTY and merciful God, Who art the strength of the weak, the refreshment of the weary, the comfort of the sad, the help of the tempted, the God of all patience and of all consolation; Thou knowest the inner weakness of our nature, how we tremble before pain, and cannot bear the cross without Thy help and support.

Help me, O eternal God, help me to possess my soul in patience, to maintain unshaken hope in Thee, to keep that childlike trust which feels a Father's heart hidden beneath the cross.

So shall I be strengthened with power according to Thy glorious might, in all patience and long-suffering.

I shall be enabled to endure pain and temptation, and in the depth of my suffering, to praise Thee with a joyful heart.

Adapted from Johann Habermann, 1516-1590

Be ye transformed by the renewing of your mind.

ROMANS xii. 2

SPEAK, Lord, for Thy servant heareth.
Grant us ears to hear,
Eyes to see,
Wills to obey,
Hearts to love;
Then declare what Thou wilt,
Reveal what Thou wilt,
Command what Thou wilt,
Demand what Thou wilt.

Christina Rossetti, 1830-1894

Because your soul was precious in My sight.

À KEMPIS

PRAY Him to give you what Scripture calls "an honest and good heart," or "a perfect heart," and, without waiting, begin at once to obey Him with the best heart you have. Any obedience is better than none.

You have to seek His face; obedience is the only way of seeing Him. All your duties are obediences. To do what He bids is to obey Him, and to obey Him is to approach Him.

John Henry Newman, Cardinal, 1801-1890

A mind content both crown and kingdom is.

ROBERT GREENE

GIVE me, O Lord, a tender conscience; a conversation discreet and affable, modest and patient, liberal and obliging; a body chaste and healthful, competency of living according to my condition, contentedness in all estates, a resigned will and mortified affections: that I may be as Thou wouldest have me, and my portion may be in the lot of the righteous, in the brightness of Thy countenance, and the glories of eternity.

Jeremy Taylor, 1613-1667

O ALMIGHTY God, eternal treasure of all good things, never let my desires of this world be greedy, nor my thoughts intemperate, nor my cares vexatious and distracting; but moderate, holy, subordinate to Thy will, the measure Thou hast appointed me.

Jeremy Taylor, 1613-1667

Most loving Lord, give me a child-like love of Thee, which may cast out all fear. E. B. PUSEY

O GOD, Who hast chosen the weak things of the world to confound the mighty, do Thou shed forth continual day upon us who watch for Thee; that our lips may praise Thee, our life may bless Thee, and our meditations glorify Thee.

Sarum Breviary

Great souls are always loyally submissive, reverent to what is over them.   CARLYLE

O LORD God everlasting, Which reignest over the kingdoms of men . . . so teach me, I humbly beseech Thee, Thy word, and so strengthen me with Thy grace that I may feed Thy people with a faithful and a true heart, and rule them prudently with power. O Lord, Thou hast set me on high. My flesh is frail and weak. If I therefore at any time forget Thee, touch my heart, O Lord, that I may again remember Thee. If I swell against Thee, pluck me down in my own conceit. . . . I acknowledge, O my King, without Thee my throne is unstable, my seat unsure, my kingdom tottering, my life uncertain. I see all things in this life subject to mutability, nothing to continue still at one stay. . . . Create therefore in me, O Lord, a new heart, and so renew my spirit that Thy law may be my study, Thy truth my delight, Thy church my care. Thy people my crown, Thy righteousness my pleasure, Thy service my government; so shall this my kingdom through Thee be established with peace.

Queen Elizabeth I, 1558-1603

[Found after her death in a little book in which she set down her thoughts about God, who, she believed, guided her.]

A vain shadow strikes the anxious with fear.

OVID

O MOST loving Father, who willest us to give thanks
for all things, to dread nothing but the loss of thee, and
to cast all our care on thee who carest for us; preserve
us from faithless fears and worldly anxieties, and grant
that no clouds of this mortal life may hide from us the
light of that love which is immortal, and which thou hast
manifested unto us in thy Son, Jesus Christ our Lord.

William Bright, 1824-1901

For a man is what he is in Thy sight, and nothing more.

À KEMPIS

GRANT me, O Lord, to know what I ought to know, to love what I ought to love, to praise what delights Thee most, to value what is precious in Thy sight, to hate what is offensive to Thee.

Do not suffer me to judge according to the sight of my eyes, nor to pass sentence according to the hearing of the ears of ignorant men; but to discern with a true judgment between things visible and spiritual, and above all things always to inquire what is the good pleasure of Thy will.

Thomas à Kempis, 1380-1471

Through the thanksgiving of many, redound to the glory of God.   II CORINTHIANS iv. 15

Lord, with what courage and delight
    I do each thing,
When Thy least breath sustains my wing!
    I shine and move
    Like those above,
    And, with much gladness
    Quitting sadness,
Make me fair days of every night.

Affliction thus mere pleasure is;
    And hap what will,
If Thou be in't, 'tis welcome still.
    But since Thy rays
    In sunny days
    Thou dost thus lend
    And freely spend,
Ah! what shall I return for this.

O that I were all soul! that Thou
    Wouldst make each part
Of this poor, sinful frame, pure heart!
    This would I drown
    My single one
    And to Thy praise
    A consort raise
Of hallelujahs here below.

Henry Vaughan, 1622-1695

That was the true Light, which lighteth every man that cometh into the world. JOHN i. 9

Give me, O Lord, purity of lips, a clean and innocent heart; humility, fortitude, patience.

Give me the Spirit of wisdom and understanding, the Spirit of counsel and strength, the Spirit of knowledge and godliness, and of Thy fear.

Make me ever to seek Thy face with all my heart, all my soul, all my mind; grant me to have a contrite and humble heart in Thy Presence.

Most high, eternal and ineffable Wisdom, drive away from me the darkness of blindness and ignorance; most high and eternal Strength, deliver me; most high and eternal Light, illuminate me; most high and infinite Mercy, have mercy on me.

Gallican Liturgy, ninth century

If there be any good in thee, believe that there is much more in others—that so thou mayest preserve humility within thee. À KEMPIS

FINALLY, brethren, whatsoever things are true, whatsoever things are honest, whatsoever things are just, whatsoever things are pure, whatsoever things are lovely, whatsoever things are of good report; if there be any virtue, and if there be any praise, think on these things.

Philippians, iv. 8-9

THREE

SON OF GOD

I can do all things through Christ who strengtheneth me. *Philippians* iv. 13

That which was written was upright, even words of truth.

ECCLESIASTES xii. 10

RICHARD, run ryghte
In Life's race:
Christ thy myghte,
His thy grace;
His thy lyghte
Round thy wayes
All thy dayes.

*B. C. Boulter: for the baptism of Richard
Southby, grandson of Lady Southby*

Peace let us seek, to steadfast things attune calm ex-
pectations.   WORDSWORTH

GRANT me, O most merciful Jesus, Thy grace, that it may be with me, and labour with me, and abide with me even to the end.

Give me grace ever to desire and to will what is most acceptable to Thee, and most pleasing in Thy sight. Let Thy Will be mine, and let my will ever follow Thine, and fully accord with it.

Let there be between Thee and me but one will, so that I may love what Thou lovest and abhor what Thou hatest; and let me not be able to will anything which Thou dost not will, nor to dislike anything which Thou dost will.

Grant that I may die to all things which are on the earth, and for Thy sake love to be despised, and to be unknown in the world.

Grant to me, above all things to be desired, that I may rest in Thee, and that my heart may find its peace in Thee. Thou art the peace of my heart, Thou its sole repose; out of Thee all things are hard and unquiet.

In this very peace, that is in Thyself, the Sole, the Supreme, the Eternal Good, I will sleep and take my rest.

Thomas à Kempis, 1380-1471

In chains . . . they shall make supplication unto thee.
                                        ISAIAH xlv. 14

O LORD my God. I have hoped in Thee,
O dear Jesus, set me free.
Though hard the chains that fasten me,
And sore my lot, yet I long for Thee
I languish and groaning bend my knee,
Adoring, imploring, O set me free.

Mary, Queen of Scots (1542-1587),
on the eve of her execution

I long to bring Thee into my house.

O HOLY Christ,
O Lord of Light,
Succour me now
In my affright.

O Holy Christ,
Ride fast and rout
My foes that ring
My soul about.

O Holy Christ,
Now in this hour,
Keep tryst with me
And be my tower.

Thought to be an ancient Gaelic prayer

If we live in the Spirit, let us also walk in the Spirit.
GALATIANS V. 25

O MOST merciful Redeemer,
Friend and Brother,
May we know Thee more clearly,
Love Thee more dearly,
And follow Thee more nearly;
For Thine own sake.

Richard of Chichester, fourteenth century

O LORD, grant all who contend for the faith, never to
injure it by clamor and impatience; but, speaking Thy
precious truth in love, so to present it that it may be
loved, and that men may see in it Thy goodness and Thy
beauty.

Adapted from William Bright, 1824-1901

Son, I came down from Heaven for your salvation.

Á KEMPIS

O HOLY Child of Bethlehem!
Descend to us, we pray;
Cast out our sin, and enter in,
Be born in us to-day.
We hear the Christmas angels
The great glad tidings tell;
Oh come to us, abide with us,
Our Lord Emmanuel.

Phillips Brooks, Bishop, 1835-1893

WHAT can I give him
Poor as I am?
If I were a shepherd
I would bring a lamb;
If I were a wise man
I would do my part;
Yet what can I give him—
Give my heart.

Christina Rossetti, 1830-1894

Follow my Voice, and you shall be able to enjoy much peace. À KEMPIS

His Kingdom come. For this we pray in vain,
Unless he does in our affections reign.
Absurd it were to wish for such a King,
And not obedience to his sceptre bring,
Whose yoke is easy, and his burden light,
His service freedom, and his judgments right.

Edmund Waller, 1606-1687

Do good to me, O Lord, for Thy name's sake.

LUTHER

WHEN, as a child, I laughed and wept,
    Time crept.
When, as a youth, I dreamed and talked,
    Time walked.
When I became a full-grown man,
    Time ran.
And later, as I older grew,
    Time flew.
Soon I shall find, while travelling on,
    Time gone.
Will Christ have saved my soul
    By then?
    Amen.

Inscribed on the door of a grandfather
clock in Chester Cathedral

WATCH with me, Jesus, in my loneliness,
Though others say me Nay, yet say Thou Yes;
Though others pass me by, stop Thou to bless.

Christina Rossetti, 1830-1894

FOUR

INNER PEACE

That peace which the world cannot give.

Book of Common Prayer

God the first garden made, and the first city Cain.

COWLEY

From LINES IN KENSINGTON GARDENS

Calm soul of all things! make it mine
To feel, amid the city's jar,
That there abides a peace of thine,
Man did not make, and cannot mar!

The will to neither strive nor cry,
The power to feel with others give!
Calm, calm me more! nor let me die
Before I have begun to live.

Matthew Arnold, 1822-1888

*And that ye study to be quiet, and to do your own
business.*   I THESSALONIANS iv. 11

O Lord, my Maker and Protector, who hast graciously
sent me into this world to work out my salvation, enable
me to drive from me all such unquiet and perplex-
ing thoughts as may mislead or hinder me in the practice
of those duties which Thou hast required.

When I behold the works of thy hands, and consider
the course of thy providence, give me grace always to
remember that thy thoughts are not my thoughts, nor thy
ways my ways.

And while it shall please thee to continue me in this
world, where much is to be done, and little to be known,
teach me by thy Holy Spirit, to withdraw my mind from
unprofitable and dangerous enquiries, from difficulties
vainly curious, and doubts impossible to be solved.

Let me rejoice in the light which Thou hast imparted,
let me serve Thee with active zeal and humble confidence,
and wait with patient expectation for the time in which
the soul which Thou receivest shall be satisfied with
knowledge. Grant this, O Lord, for Jesus Christ's sake.

Samuel Johnson, 1709-1784

In singleness of your heart, as unto Christ.

EPHESIANS vi. 5

How blest thy creature is, O God,
  When with a single eye,
He views the lustre of thy Word,
  The day-spring from on high!

William Cowper, 1731-1800

Consecrate yourselves today to the Lord.

EXODUS xxxii. 29

ETERNAL God, who committest to us the swift and solemn trust of life; since we know not what a day may bring forth, but only that the hour for serving Thee is always present, may we wake to the instant claims of Thy holy will; not waiting for tomorrow, but yielding today.

Lay to rest, by the persuasion of Thy spirit, the resistance of our passion, indolence, or fear. Consecrate with Thy presence the way our feet may go; and the humblest work will shine, and the roughest places be made plain.

Lift us above unrighteous anger and mistrust into faith and hope and charity by a simple and steadfast reliance on Thy sure will. In all things draw us to the mind of Christ, that Thy lost image may be traced again, and Thou mayest own us as at one with Him and Thee.

James Martineau, 1805-1900

Purge your conscience from dead works to serve the living God. HEBREWS ix. 14

I NEED Thee to teach me day by day, according to each day's opportunities and needs. Give me, O my Lord, that purity of conscience which alone can receive, which alone can improve Thy inspirations.

My ears are dull, so that I cannot hear Thy voice. My eyes are dim, so that I cannot see Thy tokens. Thou alone canst quicken my hearing, and purge my sight, and cleanse and renew my heart.

Teach me to sit at Thy feet, and to hear Thy word.

John Henry Newman, Cardinal, 1801-1890

Guided by faith and matchless fortitude.

MILTON

O LORD, help me to understand that You ain't gwine to let nuthin' come my way that You and me together can't handle.

Repeated by a Negro boy who was running a losing race:

LAWD, You pick 'em up, and I'll put 'em down. You pick 'em up, and I'll put 'em down. . . .

Negro Prayers

Light is the shadow of God.

17TH-CENTURY SUNDIAL INSCRIPTION

I DO not ask, O Lord, that life may be
      A pleasant road;
I do not ask that Thou wouldst take from me
      Aught of its load;

I do not ask that flowers should always spring
      Beneath my feet;
I know too well the poison and the sting
      Of things too sweet.

For one thing only, Lord, dear Lord, I plead,
      Lead me aright—
Though strength should falter, and though heart
      should bleed—
      Through Peace to Light.

I do not ask, O Lord, that Thou shouldst shed
      Full radiance here;
Give but a ray of peace, that I may tread
      Without a fear.

I do not ask my cross to understand,
      My way to see—
Better in darkness just to feel Thy hand
      And follow Thee.

Joy is like restless day; but peace divine
      Like quiet night:
Lead me, O Lord—till perfect Day shall shine,
      Through Peace to Light.

Adelaide Anne Procter, 1825-1864

Every man's task is his life-preserver.

EMERSON

O Lord, Thou knowest how busy I must be this day. If I forget Thee, do not Thou forget me. . . . March on, boys!

Sir Jacob Astley, on his knees before the Battle of Edgehill, 1642

What's midnight doubt before the dayspring's Faith?

O MERCIFUL God, be Thou unto me a strong tower of defence, I humbly entreat Thee. Give me grace to await Thy leisure, and patiently to bear what Thou doest unto me; nothing doubting or mistrusting Thy goodness towards me, for Thou knowest what is good for me better than I do. Therefore do with me in all things what Thou wilt; only arm me, I beseech Thee, with Thine armour, that I may stand fast; above all things, taking to me the shield of faith; praying always that I may refer myself wholly to Thy will, abiding Thy pleasure, and comforting myself in those troubles which it shall please Thee to send me, seeing such troubles are profitable for me; and I am assuredly persuaded that all Thou doest cannot but be well; and unto Thee be all honour and glory.

Lady Jane Grey, 1537-1554

By all means use sometimes to be alone!
Salute thyself! See what thy soul doth wear!

HERBERT

I THANK Thee, Lord, for knowing me better than I know myself, and for letting me know myself better than others know me.

Make me, I pray Thee, better than they suppose, and forgive me what they do not know.

Attributed to Abu Bekr, 572(?)-634, father-in-law of Mohammed and first calif of Islam. (It is said that he recited it when he heard his people praising him.)

The principal part of faith is patience.

GEORGE MACDONALD

TAKE from us, O God, all tediousness of spirit, all impatience and unquietness. Let us possess ourselves in patience . . . through Jesus Christ our Lord.

Jeremy Taylor, 1613-1667

As the high service pledges now, now pleads.

WORDSWORTH

DEAR Lord and Father of mankind,
    Forgive our foolish ways!
Re-clothe us in our rightful mind,
In purer lives Thy service find,
    In deeper reverence praise.

In simple trust like theirs who heard,
    Beside the Syrian sea,
The gracious calling of the Lord,
Let us, like them, without a word
    Rise up and follow Thee.

O Sabbath rest by Galilee!
    O calm of hills above,
Where Jesus knelt to share with Thee
The silence of eternity,
    Interpreted by love.

Drop Thy still dews of quietness,
    Till all our strivings cease:
Take from our souls the strain and stress,
And let our ordered lives confess
    The beauty of Thy peace.

Breathe through the heats of our desire
    Thy coolness and Thy balm;
Let sense be dumb, let flesh retire;
Speak through the earthquake, wind, and fire,
    O still small voice of calm!

John Greenleaf Whittier, 1807-1892

Flattery corrupts both the receiver and giver.

FOR THE CLEANSING OF THE HEART

STRENGTHEN me, O God, by the grace of Thy Holy
Spirit; grant me to be strengthened with might in the
inner man, and to put away from my heart all useless
anxiety and distress, and let me never be drawn aside by
various longings after anything whatever, whether it be
worthless or precious; but may I regard all things as passing away, and myself as passing away with them.

For nothing is lasting under the sun, for all things are
vanity and vexation of spirit. O, how wise is he who thus
regards them.

Grant me, O Lord, heavenly wisdom, that I may learn
to seek Thee above all things, and to understand all other
things as they are, according to the order of Thy wisdom.

Grant me prudently to avoid the one who flatters me,
and patiently to bear with the one who contradicts me;
for it is a mark of great wisdom not to be moved by every
wind of words, nor to give ear to the wicked flattery of
the siren; for thus we shall go on securely in the course
we have begun.

Thomas à Kempis, 1380-1471

There is surely a piece of Divinity in us, something that was before the elements, and owes no homage to the sun.

SIR THOMAS BROWNE

VIEW ME, LORD, A WORK OF THINE

VIEW me, Lord, a work of Thine:
Shall I then lie drown'd in night?
Might Thy grace in me but shine,
I should seem made all of light.

But my soul still surfeits so
On the poisoned baits of sin,
That I strange and ugly grow,
All is dark and foul within.

Cleanse me, Lord, that I may kneel
At Thine altar, pure and white:
They that once Thy mercies feel,
Gaze no more on earth's delight.

Worldly joys like shadows fade,
When the heav'nly light appears;
But the cov'nants Thou hast made,
Endless, know nor days, nor years.

In Thy word, Lord, is my trust,
To Thy mercies fast I fly;
Though I am but clay and dust,
Yet Thy grace can lift me high.

Thomas Campion, 1567-1620

FIVE

GOD'S GRACE

Where sin abounded, grace did much more abound.

Romans v. 20

This ought to be your state, if you desire to walk with Me. À KEMPIS

LORD, I am no hero, I have been careless, cowardly, sometimes all but mutinous. Punishment I have deserved, I deny it not. But a traitor I have never been; a deserter I have never been. I have tried to fight on Thy side in Thy battle against evil.

I have tried to do the duty which lay nearest me; and to leave whatever Thou didst commit to my charge a little better than I found it.

I have not been good, but at least I have tried to be good. Take the will for the deed, good Lord.

Strike not my unworthy name off the roll-call . . . which is the blessed company of all faithful people . . . even though I stand lowest and last upon the list. Amen.

Charles Kingsley, Canon, 1819-1875

Happy shalt thou be, and it shall be well with thee.

PSALM CXXVIII. 2

THE CELESTIAL SURGEON

IF I have faltered more or less
In my great task of happiness;
If I have moved among my race
And shown no glorious morning face;
If beams from happy human eyes
Have moved me not; if morning skies,
Books, and my food, and summer rain
Knocked on my sullen heart in vain:
Lord, thy most pointed pleasure take
And stab my spirit broad awake;
Or, Lord, if too obdurate I,
Choose thou, before that spirit die,
A piercing pain, a killing sin,
And to my dead heart run them in!

Robert Louis Stevenson, 1850-1894

Who will not suffer you to be tempted above that ye
are able; but will with the temptation also make a way
to escape.   I CORINTHIANS X. 13

GIVE me, O Lord,
A steadfast heart, which no unworthy affection may drag
    downwards;
Give me an unconquered heart, which no tribulation can
    wear out;
Give me an upright heart, which no unworthy purpose
    may tempt aside.

St. Thomas Aquinas, c. 1225-1274

O GOD, by Thy mercy strengthen us who lie exposed
to the rough storms of troubles and temptations. Help
us against our own negligence and cowardice, and defend
us from the treachery of our unfaithful hearts. Succour us, we beseech Thee, and bring us to Thy safe
haven of peace and felicity.

St. Augustine, 354-430

Conscience is the voice of the soul; the passions are the voice of the body.   ROUSSEAU

O FATHER, calm the turbulence of our passions; quiet the throbbing of our hopes; repress the waywardness of our wills; direct the motions of our affections; and sanctify the varieties of our lot.

Be Thou all in all to us; and may all things earthly, while we bend them to our growth in grace, and to the work of blessing, dwell lightly in our hearts, so that we may readily, or even joyfully, give up whatever Thou dost ask for.

May we seek first Thy kingdom and righteousness; resting assured that then all things needful shall be added unto us.

Father, pardon our past ingratitude and disobedience; and purify us, whether by Thy gentler or Thy sterner dealings, till we have done Thy will on earth, and Thou removest us to Thine own presence with the redeemed in heaven.

Mary Carpenter, 1807-1887

In the multitude of thy mercy hear me, in the truth of thy salvation.   PSALM lxix. 13

O MERCIFUL God, full of compassion, long-suffering and of great pity, make me earnestly repent, and heartily to be sorry for all my misdoings; make the remembrance of them so burdensome and painful that I may flee to Thee with a troubled spirit and a contrite heart; and, O merciful Lord, visit, comfort, and relieve me; excite in me true repentance; give me in this world knowledge of Thy truth and confidence in Thy mercy, and, in the world to come, life everlasting.

Strengthen me against sin, and enable me so to perform every duty that whilst I live I may serve Thee in that state to which Thou hast called me; and, at last, by a holy and happy death, be delivered from the struggles and sorrows of this life, and obtain eternal happiness, for the sake of our Lord and Saviour, Thy Son Jesus Christ.

Samuel Johnson, 1709-1784

Full of compassion, and gracious; long-suffering, and plenteous in mercy and truth.   PSALM lxxxvi. 15

O GOD, though our sins be seven, though our sins be seventy times seven, though our sins be more in number than the hairs of our head, yet give us grace in loving penitence to cast ourselves down into the depths of Thy Compassion.

Christina Rossetti, 1830-1894

A noble mind disdains not to repent.

POPE

"Jesus, thou present Saviour! Thou hast known the depths of all sorrow: Thou hast entered that black darkness where God is not, and hast uttered the cry of the forsaken. Come, Lord, and gather of the fruits of Thy travail and Thy pleading: stretch forth Thy hand, Thou who art mighty to save the uttermost . . .

"See Lord—I bring her, as they of old brought the sick and helpless, and Thou didst heal them. . . . Make her feel the presence of the living God, who beholds all the past, to whom darkness is as noonday; who is waiting now, at the eleventh hour, for her to turn to Him. . . .

"Thou—Thou wilt breathe on the dead soul, and it shall arise from the unanswering sleep of death.

"Yea, Lord, I see Thee, coming through the darkness, coming, like the morning, with healing on Thy wings. The marks of Thy agony are upon Thee—I see, I see Thou art able and willing to save—Thou wilt not let her perish for ever.

"Come, mighty Saviour! let the dead hear Thy voice; let the eyes of the blind be opened: let her see that God encompasses her; let her tremble at nothing but at the sin that cuts her off from Him. Melt the hard heart; unseal the closed lips: make her cry with her whole soul, 'Father, I have sinned. . . .'"

Dinah Morris, the Methodist, in the condemned cell of Hetty Sorrel, in Adam Bede, *by George Eliot (Mary Ann Cross, 1819-1880)*

81

Behold, I have longed after thy precepts; quicken me in thy righteousness.   PSALM CXIX. 40

I KNOW, O Lord, and do with all humility acknowledge myself an object altogether unworthy of Thy love; but sure I am, Thou art an object altogether worthy of mine.

I am not good enough to serve Thee, but Thou hast a right to the best service I can pay.

Do Thou then impart to me some of that excellence, and that shall supply my own want of worth. Help me to cease from sin according to Thy will, that I may be capable of doing Thee service according to my duty.

Enable me so to guard and govern myself, so to begin and finish my course that, when the race of life is run, I may sleep in peace and rest in Thee.

Be with me unto the end, that my sleep may be rest indeed, my rest perfect security, and that security à blessed eternity.

St. Augustine, 354-430

Whatsoever ye do, do all to the glory of God.

I CORINTHIANS X. 31

HIS PRAYER FOR ABSOLUTION

FOR those my unbaptized rhymes,
Writ in my wild unhallowed times;
For every sentence, clause, and word,
That's not inlaid with Thee, (my Lord)
Forgive me, God, and blot each line
Out of my book, that is not Thine.
But if, 'mongst all, Thou find'st here one
Worthy Thy benediction;
That one of all the rest shall be
The glory of my work, and me.

Robert Herrick, 1591-1674

*Prayer is a shield to the soul, a sacrifice to God, and a
scourge to Satan.* BUNYAN

WILT Thou forgive that sin where I begun,
    Which was my sin, though it were done before?
Wilt Thou forgive that sin, through which I run,
    And do run still: though still I do deplore?
        When Thou hast done, Thou hast not done,
        For I have more.

Wilt Thou forgive that sin by which I have won
    Others to sin, and made my sin their door?
Wilt Thou forgive that sin which I did shun
    A year, or two; but wallowed in, a score?
        When Thou hast done, Thou hast not done,
        For I have more.

I have a sin of fear, that when I've spun
    My last thread, I shall perish on the shore;
Swear by Thyself that at my death Thy Son
    Shall shine—as He shines now, and heretofore;
        And, having done that, Thou hast done,
        I fear no more.

John Donne, 1572-1631

SIX

DAY AND NIGHT

The darkness and light to thee are both alike.

Psalm cxxxix. 11

The trivial round, the common task,
Will furnish all we need to ask. . . .

JOHN KEBLE

THE day returns and brings us the petty round of irritating concerns and duties. Help us to play the man, help us to perform them with laughter and kind faces. Let cheerfulness abound with industry. Give us to go blithely on our business all this day, bring us to our resting-beds weary and content and undishonoured, and grant us in the end the gift of sleep.

Robert Louis Stevenson, 1850-1894

GRANT us, O Lord, to pass this day in gladness and in peace, without stumbling and without stain; that, reaching the eventide victorious over all temptation, we may praise Thee, the eternal God, who art blessed, and dost govern all things, world without end.

Mozarabic

He is very rich who has Him for his friend.

À KEMPIS

In the still breath of morning light,
In the dark of blackest night,
My thoughts in prayer soar freely,
Thy love divinely near me.
    Lord, keep thou ever close,
    And I shall live.

T. Y.

For thou knowest not what a day may bring forth.

PRAISED be Thou, O God, who dost make the day bright with Thy sunshine, and the night with the beams of heavenly fires. Listen now to my prayers; watch over me with Thy power; give me grace to pass all the days of my life blamelessly, free from sin and terror. For with Thee is mercy and plenteous redemption, O Lord, my God.

Greek Liturgy

And he said, My presence shall go with thee, and I will
give thee rest. EXODUS XXXIII. 14

BLESSED art Thou, O Lord our God, the God of our fathers, who turnest the shadow of death into the morning; who hast lightened mine eyes that I sleep not in death.

O Lord, blot out as a night-mist mine iniquities. Scatter my sins as a morning cloud. Grant that I may become a child of the light, and of the day. Vouchsafe to keep me this day without sin. Uphold me when I am falling, and lift me up when I am down. Preserve this day from any evil of mine, and me from the evils of the day. Let this day add some knowledge, or good deed, to yesterday.

Oh, let me hear Thy loving-kindness in the morning, for in Thee is my trust. Teach me to do the thing that pleaseth Thee, for Thou art my God. Let Thy loving Spirit lead me forth into the land of righteousness.

Lancelot Andrewes, Bishop, 1555-1626

MY PRAYER

I THANK Thee, Lord, for Thy great gift,
　　Another morn to see.
My prayer be this—that if I live
　　The day be spent for Thee.

May I do naught to thwart Thy will,
　　But seek in every way
To do what Thou would'st have me do
　　Throughout the livelong day.

May I, when eventide arrives,
　　Bring back the day to Thee
Filled to the brim with deeds of love,
　　Kindness and Charity.

My tasks well done—at eventide—
　　I then can rest in peace,
Knowing that Thou wilt bless it all,
　　I can from labour cease.

And when the Day of Life is done
　　And Deathly Night doth fall,
If I can hear Thee say "Well Done,"
　　Then sweet will be the call.

Margaret H. Hancock

In the morning make your resolution.

ALMIGHTY God, we bless and praise Thee that we have wakened to the light of another earthly day; and now we will think of what a day should be.

Our days are Thine, let them be spent for Thee.

Our days are few, let them be spent with care.

There are dark days behind us, forgive their sinfulness; there may be dark days before us, strengthen us for their trials. We pray Thee to shine on this day, the day which we may call our own.

Lord, we go about our daily work; help us to take pleasure therein. Show us clearly what our duty is; help us to be faithful in doing it. Let all we do be well done, fit for Thine eye to see.

Give us strength to do, patience to bear, let our courage never fail.

When we cannot love our work, let us think of it as Thy task, and by our true love to Thee make unlovely things shine in the light of Thy great love, through Jesus Christ our Lord.

George Dawson, 1821-1876

Gather up all my senses unto Thee.

GLORY to Thee who safe hast kept,
And hast refresh'd me whilst I slept . . .

Heaven is, dear Lord, where'er Thou art;
O never, then, from me depart. . . .

Lord, I my vows to Thee renew,
Scatter my sins as morning dew;
Guard my first springs of thought and will,
And with Thyself my spirit fill.

Direct, control, suggest, this day,
All I design, or do, or say;
That all my powers, with all their might,
In Thy sole glory may unite.

Praise God, from whom all blessings flow,
Praise Him, all creatures here below;
Praise Him above, ye heavenly host,
Praise Father, Son, and Holy Ghost.

Thomas Ken, Bishop, 1637-1711

To trust in Thee above all is the strongest comfort of all Thy servants. À KEMPIS

WE come before Thee, O Lord, in the end of Thy day with thanksgiving.

Our beloved in the far parts of earth, those who are now beginning the labours of the day what time we end them, and those with whom the sun now stands at the point of noon, bless, help, console, and prosper them.

Our guard is relieved, the service of the day is over, and the hour come to rest. We resign into Thy hands our sleeping bodies, our cold hearths and open doors. Give us to awaken with smiles, give us to labour smiling. As the sun returns in the east, so let our patience be renewed with dawn; as the sun lightens the world, so let our loving kindness make bright this house of our habitation.

Robert Louis Stevenson, 1850-1894

In him was life; and the life was the light of men.

JOHN i. 4

FOUNTAIN of light. Light, Source of Light,
  Hear our prayer.
Our dark sins put to flight,
  O seek us, kindly Light.

Whose holy strength created man,
  Whose law condemned, whose love redeemed,
Be Thou in all men Love and Law
  Omnipotent.

The labour of the day is done,
  And we are safe,
Beneath the covert of Thy shield
  We give Thee praise.

The sun hath left us, comes the dark,
  Shine forth, O Sun.
Whose light is golden on the face
  Of the angel host.

Pour down Thy radiant light
  On our dim clouded mind.
Kindle us with Thy touch
  That we may burn.

From horror, lust and fear,
  Guard Thou our sleep,
And if we sleep not, may our eyes behold
  The citizens of God.

Alcuin, 735-804, translated by
Dr. Helen Waddell

95

I will both lay me down in peace, and sleep.

PSALM iv. 8

ALMIGHTY and Everlasting God, Who commandest Thy mercy in the day time, and in the night season declarest the same: We humbly beseech Thee, Who hast preserved us this day in safety, that tonight Thou wilt guard our rest; through Jesus Christ our Lord.

Mozarabic

CLOSE now thine eyes, and rest secure;
Thy soul is safe enough, thy body sure;
   He that loves thee, He that keeps
And guards thee, never slumbers, never sleeps.
The smiling Conscience in a sleeping breast
   Has only peace, has only rest:
   The music and the mirth of kings
Are all but discords, when she sings;
   Then close thine eyes and rest secure;
No sleep so sweet as thine, no rest so sure.

Francis Quarles, 1592-1644

*He will be easily content and at rest, whose conscience is
pure.*
À KEMPIS

GRANT us Thy peace, Lord, through the coming night;
   Turn Thou for us its darkness into light;
From harm and danger keep Thy children free,
   For dark and light are both alike to Thee.

Grant us Thy peace throughout our earthly life,
   Our balm in sorrow, and our stay in strife;
Then, when Thy voice shall bid our conflict cease,
   Call us, O Lord, to Thine eternal peace.

John Ellerton, Canon, 1826-1893

Now may the good God pardon all good men!

ELIZABETH BARRETT BROWNING

O Lord, be gracious unto us! In all that we hear or see, in all that we say or do, be gracious unto us. I ask pardon of the Great God. I ask pardon at the sunset, when every sinner turns to Him. Now and for ever I ask pardon of God. O Lord, cover us from our sins, guard our children and protect our weaker friends.

Bedouin Camel-Driver's prayer at sunset

A short prayer finds its way to Heaven.

WILLIAM LANGLAND

GOOD-NIGHT, Lord;
I'm very tired,
But You were, too.

Can't say much,
But You know all;
Even that I'm yawning.

Good-night, Lord,
Secure my sleep;
See You in the morning.

C. H.

SEVEN

LOVING SERVICE

Honor all men. Love the brotherhood.

I Peter ii. 17

He does well who serves the common good rather than his own will. À KEMPIS

JESUS, the carpenter's Son, teach us to judge work only by its value to Thee. Teach us to seek prayerfully the work in which we are best fitted to serve Thy Kingdom and our fellow pilgrims. Then give us grace to labour steadfastly and with a sure content.

Help us to see that talents are not merely great gifts of mind or body, but faith, humility, gentleness, patience, goodness and all the flowers and graces of the spirit.

Help us to know that none is born without value to Thee and all have some talent that can be invested in Thy love.

Accept, O Lord, our small talent, as Thou accepted the widow's mite, and bless its use in Thy service and for Thy honour and glory and the good of all mankind.

T. T.

There may be worship without words.

LONGFELLOW

God give me work
Till my life shall end
And life
Till my work is done.

*On the grave of Winifred Holtby, Novelist,
1898-1935, at Rudston, Yorkshire*

This I desire, and whatever is wanting to me do Thou deign to supply.   À KEMPIS

O GOD, Who hast commanded that no man should be idle, give us grace to employ all our talents and faculties in the service appointed to us; that whatsoever our hand findeth to do, we may do it with our whole might.

James Martineau, 1805-1900

Redeeming the time, because the days are evil.

EPHESIANS V. 16

O ETERNAL God, who hast created me to do the work of God after the manner of men, give me Thy grace that I may be a prudent spender of my time, so that I may be profitable to the Christian commonwealth; and by discharging all my duty, may glorify Thee.

Jeremy Taylor, 1613-1667

O LORD, renew our spirits that our work may not be to us a burden, but a delight. Oh, let us not serve Thee with the spirit of bondage as slaves, but with the cheerfulness and gladness of children, delighting ourselves in Thee, and rejoicing in Thy work.

Benjamin Jenks, 1646-1724

Men ought always to pray and not faint.

LUKE xviii. 1

LORD, make me an instrument of Thy peace:
Where there is hatred, let me sow love;
Where there is injury, pardon;
Where there is discord, union;
Where there is doubt, faith;
Where there is despair, hope;
Where there is darkness, light;
Where there is sadness, joy.

St. Francis of Assisi, 1182-1226

*Yet in my walks it seems to me That the Grace of God is
in Courtesy.* BELLOC

O ALMIGHTY God, give to Thy servant a meek and
gentle spirit, that I may be slow to anger, and easy to
mercy and forgiveness.

Give me a wise and constant heart, that I may never
be moved to an intemperate anger for any injury that is
done or offered.

Lord, let me ever be courteous, and easy to be entreated;
let me never fall into a peevish or contentious spirit, but
follow peace with all men; offering forgiveness, inviting
them by courtesies, ready to confess my own errors, apt to
make amends, and desirous to be reconciled.

Let no sickness or cross accident, no employment or
weariness, make me angry or ungentle and discontented,
or unthankful, or uneasy to them that minister to me; but
in all things make me like unto the holy Jesus.

Jeremy Taylor, 1613-1667

I will not keep silence, but will recompense.

ISAIAH lxv. 6

O LORD give me strength to refrain from the unkind silence that is born of hardness of heart; the unkind silence that clouds the serenity of understanding and is the enemy of peace.

Give me strength to be the first to tender the healing word and the renewal of friendshp, that the bonds of amity and the flow of charity may be strengthened for the good of the brethren and the furthering of Thine eternal, loving purpose.

C. H.

The fear of the Lord, that is wisdom.

JOB xxviii. 28

ALMIGHTY God, the giver of wisdom, without whose help resolutions are vain, without whose blessing study is ineffectual; enable me, if it be Thy will, to attain such knowledge as may qualify me to direct the doubtful, and instruct the ignorant; to prevent wrongs and terminate contentions; and grant that I may use that knowledge which I shall attain, to Thy glory and my own salvation, for Jesus Christ's sake.

Samuel Johnson, 1709-1784

To shew forth thy loving-kindness in the morning, and thy faithfulness every night. PSALM XCII. 2

BE pleased, O Lord, to remember my friends, all that have prayed for me, and all that have done me good.

Do Thou good to them and return all their kindness double into their own bosom, rewarding them with blessings, and sanctifying them with Thy graces, and bringing them to glory. . . .

Let all my family and kindred, my neighbours and acquaintance receive the benefit of my prayers, and the blessings of God; the comforts and supports of Thy providence, and the sanctification of Thy Spirit.

Jeremy Taylor, 1613-1667

By the which will we are sanctified.

HEBREWS X. 10

A LOVER'S PRAYER

O GOD of earth and heaven,
And the waters that cover the sea;
Bestow on us Thy leaven,
And give my love to me.

T. T.

See whether it be well with thy brethren.

O God, Father of the forsaken, the Help of the weak, the Supplier of the needy; who teachest us that love towards the race of man is the bond of perfectness, and the imitation of Thy blessed Self; open and touch our hearts, that we may see and do, both for this world and that which is to come, the things which belong to our peace.

7th Earl of Shaftesbury, 1801-1885

Bestow on me, O Lord, a genial spirit and unwearied forbearance; a mild, loving, patient heart; kindly looks, pleasant, cordial speech and manners in the intercourse of daily life; that I may give offence to none, but as much as in me lies live in charity with all men.

Johann Arndt, 1555-1621

O God, who of Thy great love to this world, didst reconcile earth to heaven through Thine Only-Begotten Son; grant that we, who by the darkness of our sins are turned aside from brotherly love, may by Thy light shed forth in our souls Thine own sweetness and embrace our friends in Thee, forgiving our enemies, even as Thou, for Thy Son's sake, dost forgive us.

Mozarabic

A generous prayer is never presented in vain.

STEVENSON

O DIVINE Master, grant that I may not so much seek
To be consoled, as to console;
To be understood, as to understand;
To be loved, as to love;
For it is in giving that we receive,
It is in pardoning that we are pardoned,
And it is in dying that we are born
To Eternal Life.

St. Francis of Assisi, 1182-1226

*O give me light to see, a heart to choose with, and power
to do thy Will, O God.* THOMAS WILSON

O Lord, the Lord whose ways are right, keep us in
Thy mercy from lip-service and empty forms; from having
a name that we live, but being dead.

Help us to worship Thee by righteous deeds and lives
of holiness; that our prayer also may be set forth in Thy
sight as the incense, and the lifting up of our hands be
as an evening sacrifice.

Christina Rossetti, 1830-1894

God, my Creator, stand by my side,
Keep Thou the door of my lips,
Guard Thou my hands,
O Lord of Light.

Accadian

The still small voice of gratitude.

GRAY

My prayers and alms, imperfect and defiled,
Were but the feeble efforts of a child;
Howe'er performed, it was their brightest part,
That they proceeded from a grateful heart.

William Cowper, 1731-1800

*No sound ought to be heard in the church but the heal-
ing voice of Christian charity.*   BURKE

O GOD, make the door of this house wide enough to
receive all who need human love and fellowship; narrow
enough to shut out all envy, pride and strife.

Make its threshold smooth enough to be no stumbling-
block to children, nor to straying feet, but rugged and
strong enough to turn back the tempter's power. God
make the door of this house the gateway to Thine eternal
kingdom.

Ruined St. Stephen's Walbrook, London

The nobility of labor—the long pedigree of toil.

LONGFELLOW

O Lord God, when Thou givest to Thy servants to endeavour any great matter, grant us also to know that it is not the beginning but the continuing of the same until it be thoroughly finished which yieldeth the true glory.

Sir Francis Drake, 1540-1596

It is godlike for mortal to assist mortal.

PLINY THE ELDER

IF there be some weaker one,
Give me strength to help him on;
If a blinder soul there be,
Let me guide him nearer Thee;
Make my mortal dreams come true
With the work I fain would do;
Clothe with life the weak intent,
Let me be the thing I meant;
Let me find in Thy employ
Peace that dearer is than joy;
Out of self to love be led,
And to heaven acclimated,
Until all things sweet and good
Seem my natural habitude.

John Greenleaf Whittier, 1807-1892

Forgive how I have failed, who saw'st me strive.

LYTTON

TEACH us, good Lord, to serve Thee as Thou deservest:
To give and not to count the cost;
To fight and not to heed the wounds;
To toil and not to seek for rest;
To labour and not to ask for any reward
Save that of knowing that we do Thy will.

St. Ignatius Loyola, 1491-1556

. . . a man's reach should exceed his grasp, or what's a
heaven for? **BROWNING**

GIVE me an heart that beats
In all its pulses with the common heart
Of human kind, which the same things make glad,
The same make sorry! Give me grace enough
Even in their first beginnings to detect
The endeavours which the proud heart still is making
To cut itself from off the common root,
To set itself upon a private base,
To have wherein to glory of its own,
Beside the common glory of the kind!
Each such attempt in all its hateful pride
And meanness, give me to detect and loathe,—
A man, and claiming fellowship with men!

Richard C. Trench, Archbishop, 1807-1886

O LORD,
What shall I do to gain eternal life?
"Discharge aright
The simple dues with which each day is rife;
Yea, with thy might."

Friedrich von Schiller, 1775-1854

Flight is not our only weapon, but patient endurance and true humility, whereby we become stronger than all our enemies. À KEMPIS

GOD, Who has made all creatures for Thy own Glory, and has destined all the things of this world for the service of mankind, bless, we pray Thee, this machine built for our travel, that it may serve—without loss or danger—for spreading ever more widely the praise and glory of Thy name, and for the quicker dispatch of the world's affairs; and may foster in the hearts of those who travel in it a yearning for the things above, through Christ our Lord.

Prayer displayed in Aer Lingus passenger planes

And . . . giving all diligence, add to your faith virtue;
and to virtue knowledge.   II PETER i. 5

O ETERNAL God, Thou Fountain of justice, mercy and
benediction, who by my education and other effects of
Thy Providence hast called me to this profession, that by
my industy I may in my small proportion work together
for the good of myself and others: I humbly beg Thy
grace to guide me in my intention, and in the transaction
of my affairs, so that I may be diligent, just, and faithful; and give me Thy favour, that this my labour may
be accepted by Thee as part of my necessary duty: and
give me Thy blessing to assist and prosper me in my calling, to such measures as Thou shalt in mercy choose for
me: and be pleased to let Thy Holy Spirit be for ever
present with me, that I may never be given to covetous-
ness and sordid appetites, to lying and falsehood, or any
other base, indirect and beggarly arts; but give me pru-
dence, honesty, and Christian sincerity, that my Trade may
be sanctified by my Religion, my labour by my intention
and Thy blessing; that, when I have done my portion
of work Thou hast allotted me, and improved the talent
Thou hast intrusted to me, and served the Commonwealth in my capacity, I may receive the mighty price
of my high calling, which I expect and beg, in the portion
and inheritance of the ever-blessed Saviour and Redeemer
Jesus.

                              Jeremy Taylor, 1613-1667

This is the victory that overcometh the world.

I JOHN V. 4

AN ATHLETE'S PRAYER

HELP me to play the game, dear Lord,
   With all my might and main;
Grant me the courage born of right.
   A heart to stand the strain.

Send me a sense of humour, Lord,
   To laugh when victory's mine—
To laugh, if I should meet defeat,
   Without a fret or whine.

Give me the grace to follow rules,
   Confess when I am wrong,
When silence or the other thing
   Wins plaudits from the throng.

When foes are tough and fighting fierce
   And I am getting weak,
Dear God, don't ever let me show
   A broad, bright yellow streak.

And teach me, Lord, life's game to play
   Just one day at a time—
With Thee as coach and trainer, Lord,
   Real victory must be mine.

           Frederick D. Tyner

Come unto me, all ye that labour and are heavy laden,
and I will give you rest. MATTHEW xi. 28

A HOUSEWIFE'S PRAYER

THE privilege of yielding uno Thee,
The day with all it holds in store for me,
In every act to do it as for Thee.
    A housewife's humble prayer.

To start the day with all its duties small
And claim Thy strength and promised help in all.
To know that Thou wilt answer ere I call.
    A housewife's answered prayer.

To offer unto Thee when night draws nigh
A humble worship—penitential sigh.
To have Thy Blessing as Thou passest by.
    A housewife's grateful prayer.

Margaret H. Hancock

In the delight that work alone can give.

TEACH me, my God and King,
    In all things Thee to see,
And what I do in anything,
    To do it as for Thee!
All may of Thee partake,
    Nothing can be so mean,
Which with this tincture (for Thy sake)
    Will not grow bright and clean.
A servant with this clause
    Makes drudgery divine!
Who sweeps a room as for Thy laws
    Makes that and th'action fine.

George Herbert, 1593-1633

And, having done all, to stand.

O GOD our Father, let us not be content to wait and see what will happen, but give us the determination to make the right things happen.

While time is running out, save us from patience which is akin to cowardice.

Give us the courage to be either hot or cold, to stand for something, lest we fall for anything. In Jesus' name, Amen.

Dr. Peter Marshall (1902-1949), Chaplain to U.S. Congress. Used in the Senate, March 10, 1948

There must be some great truth underlying the instinct for worship. SIR OLIVER LODGE

O Lord, and Master of us all,
    Whate'er our name or sign,
We own Thy sway, we hear Thy call,
    We test our lives by Thine.

Thou judgest us; Thy purity
    Doth all our lusts condemn;
The love that draws us nearer Thee
    Is hot with wrath to them;

Our thoughts lie open to Thy sight;
    And naked to Thy glance
Our secret sins are in the light
    Of Thy pure countenance.

Yet weak and blinded though we be
    Thou dost our service own;
We bring our varying gifts to Thee,
    And Thou rejectest none.

To Thee our full humanity,
    Its joys and pains belong;
The wrong of man to man on Thee
    Inflicts a deeper wrong.

Apart from Thee all gain is loss,
    All labour vainly done;
The solemn shadow of Thy Cross
    Is better than the sun.

John Greenleaf Whittier, 1807-1892

Prayer is a study of truth—a sally of the soul into the unfound infinite.   EMERSON

TO HIS DEAR GOD

I'LL hope no more
For things that will not come:
And, if they do, they prove but cumbersome;
Wealth brings much woe:
And, since it fortunes so,
'Tis better to be poor,
Than so abound,
As to be drown'd,
Or overwhelm'd with store.

Pale care, avant!
I'll learn to be content
With that small stock Thy bounty gave or lent.
What may conduce
To my most healthful use,
Almighty God, me grant;
But that, or this,
That hurtful is
Deny Thy suppliant.

Robert Herrick, 1591-1674

How rarely we weigh our neighbour in the same balance in which we weigh ourselves. À KEMPIS

I OFFER to Thee prayers for all those whom I have in any way grieved, vexed and oppressed, by word or deed, knowingly or unknowingly, that Thou mayest equally forgive us all our sins, and all our offences against each other.

Take away, O Lord, from our hearts all suspiciousness, indignation, anger and contention, and whatever is likely to wound charity and to lessen brotherly love.

Have mercy, O Lord, have mercy on those who seek Thy mercy; give grace to the needy; make us so to live that we may be found worthy to enjoy the fruits of Thy grace.

Thomas à Kempis, 1380-1471

EIGHT

THE NATION

Blessed are the people who have the Lord for their God. *Psalm* cxliv. 15

Blessed are the valiant that have lived in the Lord.

CARLYLE

ARM me, O Thou God of battles, with courage this day, that I may not fall before my enemies. The quarrel is Thine, let the victory be Thine. Tie to my sinews the strength of David, that I may with a pebble stone strike to the earth these giants that fight against Thy truth.

So let me fight that, whether I come off lame or sound, dead or alive, I may live or die Thy soldier.

Thomas Dekker, 1570(?)-1632

I form'd them free, and free they must remain till they enthrall themselves.   MILTON

O LET Thine enemies know that Thou hast received England . . . into Thine own protection. Set a wall about it, O Lord, and ever more mightily defend it. Let it be a comfort to the afflicted, a help to the oppressed, and a defence to Thy church and people persecuted abroad. . . . Direct and go before our armies both by sea and land. Bless them and prosper them, and grant unto them Thy honourable success and victory.

Queen Elizabeth I, 1558-1603

[Written when news came that the Armada had sailed. It was read twice a week in all the churches till peace came.]

Thank God, guilt was never a rational thing.

BURKE

ALMIGHTY God, by whom alone kings reign and princes decree justice, and from whom alone cometh all counsel, wisdom, and understanding,

We, Thine unworthy servants, here gathered together in Thy name, do most humbly beseech Thee to send down the heavenly wisdom from above, to direct and guide us in all our consultations:

And grant that, we having Thy fear always before our eyes, and laying aside all private interests, prejudices, and partial affections, the result of all our counsels may be the glory of Thy blessed name, the maintenance of true religion and justice, and the safety, honour, and happiness of the King, the public welfare, peace and tranquillity of the realm, and the uniting and knitting together of the hearts of all persons and estates within the same in true Christian love and charity towards one another, Through Jesus Christ our Lord and Saviour.

The Prayer of the House of Commons

[Used at every sitting of the House, and composed by Sir Christopher Yelverton, M.P. for Northampton and Speaker of the House, some time about 1578.]

The cause of freedom is the cause of God.

WILLIAM LISLE BOWLES

For good fellowship in freedom and for those who made it possible, we give thanks.

(I have been asked by friends to include this grace, which I wrote and used as chairman of the Paternosters Club during the Battle of Britain.—C. H.)

Think, and thank God.

PROVERB

No ordinary meal—a sacrament awaits us
On our tables daily spread,
For men are risking lives on sea and land
That we may dwell in safety and be fed.

A Grace, told to me in Scotland
many years ago

He was the Word, that spake it.

THREE things are of the Evil One:

> An evil eye;
> An evil tongue;
> An evil mind.

Three things are of God, and these three are what Mary told to her Son, for she heard them in Heaven:

> The merciful word,
> The singing word,
> And the good word.

May the power of these three holy things be on all men and women of Erin for evermore, Amen.

Traditional Irish prayer

NINE

OUR CHILDREN

That our sons may grow up as the young plants, and that our daughters may be as the polished corners of the temple.

Psalm cxliv. 12

For such a child I blesse God, in whose bosom he is!
May I and mine become as this little child.   EVELYN

BLESS my children with healthful bodies, with good understandings, with the graces and gifts of Thy Spirit, with sweet dispositions and holy habits, and sanctify them throughout in their bodies and Souls and spirits, and keep them unblameable to the coming of the Lord Jesus.

Jeremy Taylor, 1613-1667

My words are spirit and life.

À KEMPIS

GOD who created me
  Nimble and light of limb,
In three elements free,
  To run, to ride, to swim:
Not when the sense is dim,
  But now from the heart of joy,
I would remember Him:
  Take the thanks of a boy.

Jesu, King and Lord,
  Whose are my foes to fight,
Gird me with Thy sword,
  Swift and sharp and bright.
Thee would I serve if I might;
  And conquer if I can,
From day-dawn till night,
  Take the strength of a man.

Spirit of Love and Truth,
  Breathing in grosser clay,
The light and flame of youth,
  Delight of men in the fray,
Wisdom in strength's decay;
  From pain, strife, wrong to be free,
This best gift I pray,
  Take my spirit to Thee.

H. C. Beeching, Canon, 1859-1919

142

Thou wilt shew me the path of life: in thy presence is
fulness of joy. PSALM XVI. 11

Saint James the Less,
We pray thee, bless
Young James' childhood days:
And, prithee, later
Saint James the Greater,
Conduct him through life's tortuous ways:
Then, less and greater, he shall bring
Smiles for our frowns, hope for our suffering.

B. C. Boulter: lines written for the baptism
of James Piercy, grandson of Lord Piercy

TEN

NATURE

The heavens declare the glory of God.

Psalm xix. 1

And for all that happens to me to give thanks.

À KEMPIS

WE thank Thee, Lord, for the glory of the late days and the excellent face of Thy sun. We thank thee for good news received. We thank Thee for the pleasures we have enjoyed and for those we have been able to confer. And now, when the clouds gather and the rain impends, permit us not to be cast down; let us not lose the savour of past mercies and past pleasures; but, like the voice of a bird singing in the rain, let grateful memory survive in the hour of darkness. If there be in front of us any painful duty, strengthen us with the grace of courage; if any act of mercy, teach us tenderness and patience.

Robert Louis Stevenson, 1850-1894

Let the universe hold its peace in Thy Presence.

À KEMPIS

O LORD, teach me to see Thy beauty in all things;
In earth and sky and sea Thy glorious majesty;
In nature, from the forest tree to the harebell stem,
The splendour of Thy works;
In animals, the perfection of Thy grace;
In the smile of a babe Thy sweet serenity;
In the loving works of man, the sanctity of toil,
And in every living thing to seek for Thy reflection.

C. H.

My God, I thank Thee, Who hast made
    The earth so bright,
So full of splendour and of joy,
    Beauty and light!
So many glorious things are here,
    Noble and right!

Adelaide Anne Procter, 1825-1864

No one without Him can understand or rightly judge anything.

À KEMPIS

THERE is no unbelief;
Whoever plants a seed beneath the sod,
And waits to see it push away the clod,
   He trusts in God.

Whoever says, when clouds are in the sky
Be patient, heart; light breaketh by and by,
   Trusts the Most High.

Whoever sees, 'neath winter's fields of snow,
The silent harvest of the future grow,
   God's power must know.

Lord Lytton, 1803-1873

Thy prayer is heard.

HE prayeth best, who loveth **best**
All things both great and small;
For the dear God who loveth us,
He made and loveth all.

Samuel Taylor Coleridge, 1772-1834

His mind was a thanksgiving to the Power that made him.　　　　　　　　　　　　　　　　WORDSWORTH

LET all the world in every corner sing,
　　　My God and King!
The heavens are not too high,
His praise may thither fly:
The earth is not too low,
His praises there may grow.
Let all the world in every corner sing,
　　　My God and King!

Let all the world in every corner sing,
　　　My God and King!
The Church with psalms must shout,
No door can keep them out:
But, above all, the heart
Must bear the longest part.
Let all the world in every corner sing,
　　　My God and King!

George Herbert, 1593-1633

In quietness and confidence shall be your strength.

ISAIAH XXX. 15

O GOD of mountains, stars, and boundless spaces!
O God of Freedom and of joyous hearts!
When Thy Face looketh forth from all men's faces,
There will be room enough in crowded marts:
Brood Thou around me, and the noise is o'er;
Thy universe my closet with shut door.

George Macdonald, 1824-1905

They please Him best who labor most to do in peace His Will.
WORDSWORTH

O LORD, who hast given us Thy summer sun to gladden us with his light and to ripen the fruits of the earth for our support, and who biddest him to set when his work is done, that he may rise again to-morrow; give Thy blessing to us Thy servants, that the lesson of the works of Thy hand may be learnt by us Thy living works, and that we may run our course like the sun which is now gone from us.

Let us rise early and go late to rest, being ever busy and zealous in doing Thy will. Let our light shine before men, that they may glorify Thee, our Heavenly Father. Let us do good all our days, and be useful to and comfort others. And let us finish our course in faith, that we too may rise again to a course which shall never end.

Thomas Arnold, 1795-1842

O MOST high, almighty, good Lord God, to Thee belong praise, glory, honour, and all blessing!

Praised be my Lord God with all His creatures, and specially our brother the sun, who brings us the day and who brings us the light; fair is he and shines with a very great splendour: O Lord, he signifies to us Thee!

Praised be my Lord for our sister the moon, and for the stars, the which He has set clear and lovely in heaven.

Praised be my Lord for our brother the wind, and for the air and cloud, calms and all weather by the which Thou upholdest life in all creatures.

Praised be my Lord for our sister water, who is very serviceable unto us and humble and precious and clean.

Praised be my Lord for our brother fire, through whom Thou givest us light in the darkness; and he is bright and pleasant and very mighty and strong.

Praised be my Lord for our mother the earth, the which doth sustain us and keep us, and bringeth forth divers fruits and flowers of many colours, and grass.

Praised be my Lord for all those who pardon one another for His love's sake, and who endure weakness and tribulation; blessed are they who peaceably shall endure, for Thou, O most Highest, shalt give them a crown.

Praised be my Lord for our sister, the death of the body, from which no man escapeth. Woe to him who dieth in mortal sin! Blessed are they who are found walking by Thy most holy will, for the second death shall have no power to do them harm.

Praise ye and bless the Lord, and give thanks unto Him and serve Him with great humility.

St. Francis of Assisi, 1182-1226

154

ELEVEN

THE THANKFUL HEART

Every day will I give thanks unto thee.

Psalm cxlv. 2

What shall I render . . . for love so remarkable as this?

À KEMPIS

O Lord of heaven, and earth, and sea,
To Thee all praise and glory be!
How shall we show our love to Thee,
    Giver of all?

For peaceful homes, and healthful days,
For all the blessings earth displays,
We owe Thee thankfulness and praise,
    Giver of all!

Christopher Wordsworth, Bishop,
1807-1885

Maker and High Priest,
I ask Thee not my joys to multiply,
Only to make me worthier of the least.

Elizabeth Barrett Browning, 1806-1861

Give to God thanks for His Grace.

À KEMPIS

WE are evil, O God, and help us to see it and amend. We are good, and help us to be better. Look down upon thy servants with a patient eye, even as Thou sendest sun and rain; look down, call upon the dry bones, quicken, enliven; recreate in us the soul of service, the spirit of peace; renew in us the sense of joy.

Robert Louis Stevenson, 1850-1894

LORD, what thou wilt command,
Hearts' gladness or hearts' grieving,
I will rejoice, believing
That both are from Thy hand.

Edouard Mörike, 1804-1875

THOU that hast given so much to me,
Give one thing more, a grateful heart.
Not thankful when it pleaseth me,
As if Thy blessings had spare days;
But such a heart, whose pulse may be
    Thy praise.

George Herbert, 1593-1633

Giving thanks always for all things.

O Lord my God, for life and reason, nurture, preservation, guidance, education; for Thy gifts of grace and nature, for Thy calling, recalling, manifold recalling me again; for Thy forbearance, long-suffering, and long long-suffering toward me, even until now; for all from whom I have received any good or help; for the use of Thy present good things; for Thy promise, and my hope, of good things to come; for all these things, and for all other, which I know, which I know not, manifest or secret, remembered or forgotten by me, I praise Thee, I bless Thee, I give Thee thanks; and I will praise, and bless, and give Thee thanks, all the days of my life.

What shall I render unto the Lord for all His benefits to me? Thou art worthy, O Lord, to receive glory, and honour, and power.

Lancelot Andrewes, Bishop, 1555-1626

It is the gift of God.

ECCLESIASTES iii. 13

TWO GIFTS

WE thank Thee, Lord, for Memory
    To live again the past;
That in remembering bygone days
    The fruits of joy shall last.

But for the power to forget
    We thank Thee even more:
The stings, the slights, the hurts, the wounds,
    Can never hurt us more.

Margaret H. Hancock

Magnify him with thanksgiving.

PSALM lxix. 30

WE thank Thee for Thy tender love
    And for Thy sheltering care;
For shadows lifted, ways made plain,
    Joyousness everywhere.

We thank Thee, too, for strength received
    To face life day by day;
For health and beauty, love and joy,
    And all that makes life gay.

We thank Thee every waking morn,
    And every sleeping eve;
For countless blessings day by day,
    Dear Lord, our thanks receive.

               Margaret H. Hancock

*O day most calm, most bright, The fruit of this, the next
world's bud.*   HERBERT

THE Sunday before his death, he rose suddenly from
his Bed or Couch, call'd for one of his Instruments, took
it into hand, and said—

> My God, My God,
> My Musick shall find thee,
> And every string
> shall have his attribute to sing.

And having tun'd it, he play'd and sung:

> The Sundays of Mans life,
> Thredded together on times string,
> Make Bracelets, to adorn the Wife
> Of the eternal glorious King:
> On Sundays, Heavens dore stands ope;
> Blessings are plentiful and rife,
> More plentiful than hope.

> *Izaak Walton,* 1593-1683, in The
> Life of George Herbert

TWELVE

HEAVEN

I saw a new heaven.

Revelation **xxi.** 1

In my Father's house are many mansions.

JOHN xiv. 2

WILL you, Father Nicholas,
Sometimes pray for me?
Will you give me too a place
In your family?
Boys and girls and sailormen
And pawnbrokers are there:
Will you, Father Nicholas,
Grant me too a share?
Then, please God, you'll lead us all
Up into His heavenly Hall.

B. C. Boulter

*God created . . . every living creature . . . and saw
that it was good.*   GENESIS i. 21

O GOD, my Master, should I gain the grace
To see Thee face to face when life is ended,
Grant that a little dog, who once pretended
That I was God, may see me face to face!

*B. C. Boulter, from the French of
Francis Jammes*

Behold the bright examples of the holy Fathers.

À KEMPIS

BLESSED are all Thy saints, O God and King, who have travelled over the tempestuous sea of this life and have made the harbour of peace and felicity. Watch over us who are still on our dangerous voyage; and remember such as lie exposed to the rough storms of trouble and temptations.

Frail is our vessel, and the ocean is wide; but as in Thy mercy Thou hast set our course, so steer the vessel of our life towards the everlasting shore of peace, and bring us at length to the quiet haven of our heart's desire, where Thou, O God, art blessed and livest and reignest for ever.

St. Augustine, 354-430

The souls of the righteous are in the hands of God.
WISDOM iii. 1

ALMIGHTY, eternal God, to whom there is never any prayer made without hope of mercy, be merciful to the souls of Thy servants departed from this world in the confession of Thy name, that they may be associated to the company of Thy saints.

Queen Elizabeth I (1558-1603),
Prayer for All Souls

The hand of God hath touched me.

JOB XIX. 21

INTO thy hands, Almighty Father, who dost will peace and purpose loving-kindness, we commend our spirits: our minds to know thee, our hearts to love thee, our wills to serve thee, for we are thine. Into thy hands, Incarnate Saviour, who hast taught us that thou art the way, the truth and the life, receive us and draw us after thee, that we may follow thy steps; enlighten and guide us, lest the night of sin and error overwhelm us; abide in us and quicken us by the power of thine indwelling. Into thy hands, O Lord the Spirit, who createst good and destroy-est evil, take us and fashion us after thine image: let thy comfort strengthen, thy grace renew, and thy fire cleanse us. Soul and body, in life and in death, in this world of shadows and in thy changeless world of light eternal, now and for ever, Father, Son, and Holy Spirit, into thy hands.

F. B. Macnutt, Canon, 1873-1949

And with a quiet mind go take thy rest.

THOMAS CREECH

O LORD, support us all the day long, until the shadows lengthen and the evening comes, and the busy world is hushed, and the fever of life is over, and our work is done. Then in thy mercy grant us a safe lodging, and a holy rest, and peace at the last.

*Used by Cardinal Newman, 1801-1890,
but thought by some to be a sixteenth-
century prayer*

For thine is the kingdom, and the power, and the glory.

MATTHEW vi. 13

BRING us, O Lord God, at our last awakening into the house and gate of heaven, to enter into that gate and dwell in that house, where there shall be no darkness nor dazzling, but one equal light; no noise nor silence, but one equal music; no fears nor hopes, but one equal possession; no ends nor beginnings, but one equal eternity; in the habitations of Thy glory and dominion world without end.

John Donne, 1572-1631

INDEX OF FIRST LINES

INDEX OF AUTHORS AND SOURCES

139-155-C-4